My Merry Christmas

ARCH® BOOK

Luke 2:1–20 for children

Written by Theresa Olive
Illustrated by Nancy Munger

CONCORDIA PUBLISHING HOUSE · SAINT LOUIS

This is my Merry Christmas Arch Book

Presented by

Date

King Caesar sent a message
From far away in Rome:
“Everyone must register
At their ancestral home.”

So Mary and Joseph of Nazareth,
A town in Galilee,
Traveled down to Bethlehem
To obey the king's decree.

Crowds of other visitors
Stayed there in Bethlehem.
The tired couple tried to find
A place with room for them.

At last, the owner of an inn
Said, "If the two of you don't mind,
You can sleep out in my barn—
It's the only place you'll find."

In the stable, God's own Son,
Named Jesus, soon was born.
Mary wrapped Him up and laid Him
In the manger's hay so warm.

Meanwhile shepherds watched their sheep
Near Bethlehem that night.
An angel suddenly appeared—
The shepherds shook with fright!

The angel said, “Fear not! I bring
Good news for everyone:
A baby’s born in Bethlehem—
Your Savior, God’s own Son!”

All at once a multitude
Of angels filled the sky,
Shining brighter than the sun
And praising God most high!

The shepherds raced to Bethlehem
And found the baby boy,
Wrapped up in His manger bed.
Their hearts were filled with joy!

The shepherds soon had spread the word
To people far and near:
"Good News! Our Savior has been born!
The Son of God is here!"

Today we still can celebrate,
In many special ways
The time when Jesus Christ was born
And slept in manger hay.

At Christmas when you decorate
Your tree with bright ____________________ lights,
(favorite color)
They twinkle like the stars that shone
On Bethlehem that night.

When carolers sing "______________________________,"
(favorite carol)
And you sing along,
You're bringing praise to God above
Just like the angels' song.

Before you eat your Christmas meal

Of ____________________ that tastes so good,
(favorite food)
Thank God for His blessings,
Like your home and friends and food.

As you open gifts like ____________________,
(favorite gift)
Or games you like to play,
Think of the gift God gave us
On that very first Christmas Day.

Christmas is a special day,
A time when we recall
The birthday of God's only Son—
The greatest gift of all!